Genre Myth

Essential Question

Why do people tell and retell myths?

Thor's Journey to Utgard

BY JAMES McNAUGHTON

ILLUSTRATED BY JARED OSTERHOLD

CHAPTER 1

THE GIANT

Thor was the greatest fighter of all the gods living in Asgard. He had a flaming beard and a fearsome temper. These made him a terrifying sight when he fought with his magic hammer, Mjollnir. The impact of its blows created thunder and lightning across the heavens.

One day, Thor set out in search of giants to battle. Kissing his family farewell, he took up his sturdy hammer. He and his friend Loki, the trickster god, passed through the Asgard gates. When the clouds were well above them, they turned for Utgard, the hall of the giant king, Utgard-Loke.

Thor and Loki walked all day, and as night fell, they approached a forest. The trees were so tall that their tops disappeared into the clouds. They knew they had reached Giant Land. It was cold, and an eerie mist had begun to wind its way through the trees.

Looking for somewhere to pass the night, the two friends encountered a strange building. It had no door, but a large open entrance at one end led to four long, narrow rooms and a larger side chamber. Thor and Loki were grateful for the shelter, and lying down in the longest room, they soon fell asleep.

In the middle of the night, they were woken by a violent earthquake. The building rattled, and there was a dreadful crashing, rumbling sound. A howling wind came in great gusts, bending the trees, making them groan and creak. Even Thor was frightened. He and Loki crept over the shaking floor into the side chamber. There Thor braced himself against the wall at the entrance and stood guard with his hammer at the ready.

At first light, after hours of wind, noise, and shaking, Thor decided he'd had enough. He strode outside and into the forest of quivering trees. There he found the biggest giant he had ever seen, fast asleep. The giant's snoring was making the ground shake and the forest tremble.

Thor gripped the handle of his hammer tightly. He had never seen a giant even half as large before. He ran back into the rattling building and put on his magic belt, which doubled his strength. Then he returned to the snoring giant.

Thor grasped his hammer with both hands and struck a furious blow on the side of the giant's head. The giant opened one enormous eye and mumbled, "Hmm, a leaf must have landed on me." His eye closed, and he went back to sleep.

STOP AND CHECK

Why did Thor and Loki leave their home?

Beside himself with rage, Thor struck again, this time with an even stronger blow. The giant opened both his eyes and said drowsily, “Hmm, an acorn must have fallen on me.” Then he went back to sleep, and began snoring again.

Thor was filled with righteous fury. The blows of Mjollnir had never been so lightly dismissed. He gathered all his strength, took a running leap, and swung his mightiest blow.

This time the giant grumbled and sat up. Rubbing his head, he looked up in the branches above. He said to himself, “I think a bird must have knocked a piece of moss down from the tree.” Then, looking down, he caught sight of Thor.

Thor immediately greeted the giant. “Good morning! What a nice surprise it is to meet you. May I ask your name?”

CHAPTER 2

UTGARD

The giant stretched and yawned. His breath withered the leaves on the surrounding trees. "My name is Skrymir," he said, "and you, little fellow, must be Thor. I've heard of your exploits." Looking around, he said, "I've lost a glove. Have you seen it anywhere? Ah, there it is." He reached for the funny-looking building that Thor and Loki had slept in. It was the giant's glove! The four rooms were for his fingers, and the side chamber for his thumb.

Thor called out, "Wait!" He raced into the glove to wake up Loki and get their belongings.

After Loki had introduced himself, they told Skrymir they were bound for Utgard. Skrymir stood up. Thor and Loki had to crane their heads back to look at him.

"I can tell by your expressions that you think I'm a big man," said Skrymir, "but in Utgard, there are many men as tall as I am. I suggest you keep quiet when you get there. They don't tolerate boasting from such little fellows as yourselves." Then Skrymir said good-bye, and strode rapidly away.

When Thor and Loki arrived at the walls of Utgard, they had to tilt their heads back as far as they could to see the top of them. Fortunately, the gates were open. The gods entered, making their way to the hall of the giant king, Utgard-Loke. The massive hall was a forbidding sight. The rumbling voices and gales of laughter coming from within sounded fearsome. However, Thor and Loki were valiant gods, so they entered.

Inside the hall a group of massive giants sat at two long tables that met in a V at the end. At the sight of Thor and Loki, the giants fell silent. The two gods approached the king, Utgard-Loke. They saluted him with great respect and introduced themselves.

Utgard-Loke smiled scornfully and spoke to the uninvited guests. "Little fellows, you have much audacity to come here. You might be who you say you are, but I'm not convinced. Prove that you are more than you appear."

Thor asked bravely, "How shall we do that?"

The king replied, "Show me that you are good at something, and I will allow you to remain here."

Loki stepped forward. "I can eat faster than anyone else. I am willing to prove it, if anyone here has the courage to compete against me."

Utgard-Loke laughed at the brave little god. "Very well, if you can beat our champion eater, I will be very impressed!"

A giant from the back of the hall stomped forward. A long wooden trough filled with meat was set on the floor.

"You will start at opposite ends," said Utgard-Loke to Loki and the giant. "The first one to eat his way to the middle will be the winner. Ready? Go!"

Loki started at one end, and the giant at the other. The giants bellowed and stamped their feet while the two ate and ate.

Loki ate furiously, using both hands. The giant was casual, rather delicately using only his thumb and forefinger. Within a few minutes, they met in the middle of the trough. But while Loki had eaten only the meat, the giant had eaten the bones and trough as well.

"Who is the loser?" Utgard-Loke asked the occupants of the great hall.

With much cheering and table-thumping, the giants declared Loki the loser.

STOP AND CHECK

Why did Loki compete in an eating contest?

CHAPTER 3

MORE CHALLENGES

Utgard-Loke looked down at Thor and asked, "Well, little man, are you good at anything?"

Thor knew that he had to impress the giants. He answered, "I'm known for my mighty thirst. I can drink mountain streams dry."

Utgard-Loke handed Thor a drinking horn brimming with water. "A good drinker can empty this horn in one draft," he said, "an average drinker in two, and a feeble drinker in three."

Thor drank long and deep, but when he set the horn down, it was still full.

Thor took a huge breath and drank again. He drank until he could drink no more, but the water level hardly changed.

The giants began to bang their fists on the tables.

Thor took three deep breaths and drank once more. Finally, with his breath exploding from his lungs, he set the horn down.

"Well, at least the horn can now be carried without spilling," laughed Utgard-Loke.

The giants roared with laughter.

"I suggest you try something easier," said Utgard-Loke. He gestured to his black cat, which was curled up asleep at his feet. "Why don't you try lifting this cat?"

Thor bent down and went to sweep the cat up with one hand. It was surprisingly heavy. He used both hands, but the cat seemed cemented to the ground. Thor crouched over the creature, locked his hands underneath it, and braced himself against the ground. Then he applied all his strength, but the cat didn't budge.

Thor let out his breath, stood up, and walked around, loosening his muscles. He knelt down over the sleeping cat and, with a tremendous heave, he tried again to pick it up. His muscles rippled and his face turned crimson. His veins stood out like ropes. Finally a paw lifted off the ground, but a second later it dropped back to the ground and Thor collapsed.

Furious at the giants' derisive laughter, Thor yelled, "I'm the finest wrestler in Asgard and can wrestle anyone!"

The giants shook their heads. They muttered to each other, "Who would be weak enough to make a fair contest?"

"My old nurse, Eli, would make a good match," said Utgard-Loke. "Bring her to the hall!"

Thor was embarrassed at the sight of the skinny and hunched old crone who shuffled into the hall. He extended his hand in a friendly gesture, and at once found himself on his back at the other side of the hall. The old woman cackled and the giants howled with laughter.

Thor lunged for Eli. Locked together in a wrestlers' clinch, they circled and strained. Each searched for a point of weakness. Thor tried everything he knew, but he couldn't get the upper hand. The harder he tried, the more the old woman resisted. An hour went by. Thor finally got her in a headlock, but she twisted out of it with explosive power. The giants jeered at Thor, egging Eli on.

"Stop, it's getting late," called Utgard-Loke, holding up his hand. "We need to eat dinner. But let me just say this, Thor. I don't think you should challenge anyone else."

Thor and Loki were shown to their seats. They remained quiet and somber for the rest of the night, despite being given plenty to eat and drink.

STOP AND CHECK

Why did Thor fight Eli?

CHAPTER 4

THE TRUTH IS REVEALED

Early the next morning, Thor and Loki were preparing to leave when Utgard-Loke appeared in their chambers. He insisted they eat breakfast with him. The two friends were eager to return home, but they did not wish to offend their host. They stayed for a final feast in the giant's hall.

After they had eaten their fill, Utgard-Loke led them out through the city gates. The giant crouched down to speak with his guests, and asked, "How did you enjoy your journey to Utgard?"

"I have brought great shame upon myself," Thor replied sadly. "You must think poorly of me."

"On the contrary, if I'd known you were so steadfast," Utgard-Loke said, "I would never have allowed you to enter Utgard in the first place."

"But Loki and I failed every challenge!"

"Now that you are out of the city gates," said Utgard-Loke, "I will tell you the truth, but only on the condition that you promise never to return."

Thor frowned, but he nodded his head in agreement.

STOP AND CHECK

Why did Thor feel ashamed?

"Thor, I practiced the art of deception on you," said Utgard-Loke.

"First, I disguised myself as the giant Skrymir. When you believed you were striking his head with your hammer, you were hitting a mountain. It now has three rectangular valleys, one of them especially deep. If you had hit me, it would have been the end of my days."

The giant continued. "In each of the contests, I used magic. You were both oblivious to what was really happening. The giant who beat Loki was actually Fire, who consumes everything." Loki was astonished.

Utgard-Loke continued. "Thor, when you tried to drain the drinking horn, I could hardly believe my eyes. That drinking horn extended to the sea. Your drinking set the sea in motion, in an ebb and flow of tide."

Stunned, Thor asked, "And what of the cat?"

"The cat was actually the Midgard Serpent."

Thor shook his head. "That little cat was the serpent that encircles the world?" he asked.

"Yes. You nearly pulled its tail out of its mouth," answered Utgard-Loke. "You stretched it so much that we were terrified. If the serpent loses hold of its tail, the world will end. When the cat's paw lifted, the back of the serpent nearly touched the sky."

Thor was amazed. "And the old crone Eli?"

"Eli is Old Age, whom no one will ever defeat. No one has ever wrestled with her the way you did. That was astounding."

Utgard-Loke could see that his deception had caused Thor great anger. He reminded the god, "Now you must keep your end of the bargain. It is time for you and your friend to leave and never return."

Thor was furious. He did not want to let the king of the giants get away with such trickery.

In a terrible rage, Thor swung his hammer, but it passed through thin air. Utgard-Loke had disappeared, and so had the city, its walls, and all the other giants. The two friends stood on a desolate plain.

Respond to Reading

Summarize

Use key events from Thor's Journey to Utgard to summarize this myth. Your graphic organizer may help you.

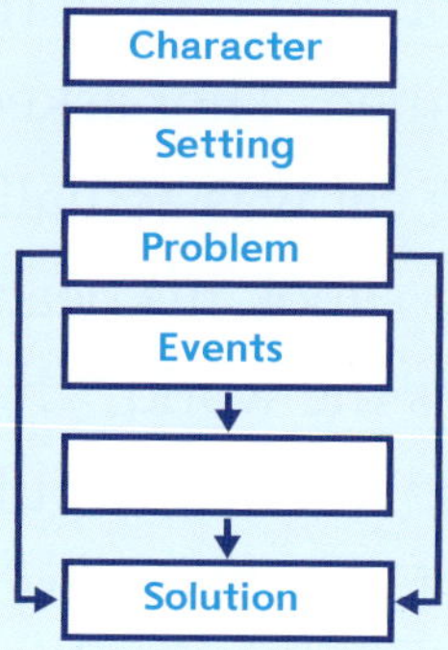

Text Evidence

1. What features of the story tell you it is a myth? GENRE

2. What is Thor's problem after he reaches Utgard? How is it solved? Use details from the text to support your answer. PROBLEM AND SOLUTION

3. The word *hammer* on page 2 comes from an old Norse word meaning "a tool with a stone head, used for hunting or in war." How does knowing the Norse origins of *hammer* help you explain its meaning as it is used now? WORD ORIGINS

4. Write about the problem Thor and Loki have in Chapter 1 and how Thor attempts to solve it. WRITE ABOUT READING

Genre Parody

Compare Texts

Read an updated myth about how Thor tames his anger.

THOR'S COUNSELOR

Thor was bored. He yearned to do battle with some giants. He ached to hurl his magic hammer, creating thunder and lightning as giants toppled like trees. And he craved the glorious feasts he would have upon his return to Asgard. He was certain his friends would throw a party.

However, when Thor suggested this plan to his anger management counselor and dietician, the counselor was not impressed.

"Thor," he said, "this is all very destructive and unhealthy. We've moved on from this kind of behavior. I suggest you simply pay the giants in Utgard a friendly visit. I'll pack some vegetarian meals and come along. With my support, you can do it."

"Yes, yes, of course," said Thor with a sigh. He knew that times had changed. He couldn't just go out and beat up giants anymore. But it was very difficult. Dejected, he walked along the walls of Asgard while his counselor prepared some salads to take with them.

"You're not taking that hammer, are you?" asked the counselor, as they were about to set off.

Thor clung to his hammer. "But it's Mjollnir! I never leave Asgard without it."

"Promise me that you'll only use it for self-defense."

Thor reluctantly agreed.

That night, after taking shelter in a strange-looking hut, they were woken by a terrible roaring and whistling noise. Thor's knuckles tightened on his hammer. He leaped up, ready for a fight.

"Oh, dear," said the counselor, "that sounds like a giant with a snoring problem. Poor fellow! I know a goddess in Asgard who can help. I'll leave him my card. We'll move on, and let him have a good night's sleep."

Thor wrung the handle of his hammer, repeating to himself, "Violence is not the answer, violence is not the answer," all the way to Utgard.

Upon their arrival, they met the king of the giants, Utgard-Loke. He challenged Thor to prove himself in a contest.

"I'm a mighty wrestler!" Thor exclaimed, forgetting himself in the excitement. "I challenge anyone in this hall to a fight."

"No, no, no," said his counselor. "How about a dancing contest?" The giants considered this in low, rumbling voices. The phrase "two left feet" came up more than once, and there was much head shaking.

"I've always preferred eating to dancing," said Utgard-Loke. He pointed to a dozen succulent pigs roasting on spits at the far end of the hall.

Thor's mouth began watering like a mountain stream. "What a fine idea!"

"Thor, you've forgotten something," the counselor reminded him. "Here. Your tofu salad."

Thor's heart sank.

"Good for you, Thor," said Utgard-Loke, trying to cheer him up. "You're in much better shape than I am."

"Why, thank you," answered Thor. It was the first compliment a giant had ever given him. He was pleasantly surprised. "I was impressed by the workmanship on the gates," he added. "How did you get that shimmering effect?"

"Well," said the king of the giants, "I'm glad you asked me that ..."

And so Thor, his counselor, and the giants had a very pleasant conversation about the work of craftsmen and artisans. When Thor left Utgard the next morning, he was invited to come back whenever he felt like getting out of Asgard.

Make Connections

Why might the character of Thor appeal to storytellers and listeners time after time? ESSENTIAL QUESTION

Compare the outcomes of both selections for Thor and Utgard-Loke. What is different? TEXT TO TEXT

Focus on Genre

Myth Myths are a form of traditional folk story, usually created to tell about gods or heroes from the past or to explain natural phenomena. Myths come from many different cultures and share certain characteristics. These include the use of characters with supernatural powers, and settings in a remote past when the world was not how it is today.

Read and Find In *Thor's Journey to Utgard,* Thor is a god who makes thunder and lightning. He can drink mountain streams dry. Utgard-Loke is a giant who uses spells to trick Thor.

Your Turn

Use the character of Thor and his attributes to create a myth that explains another natural phenomenon, such as tornadoes or hurricanes.

Work with a partner or small group to develop your ideas, making notes for a graphic story.

Plan the frames you will need to tell the myth. Then share the tasks of drawing, writing, and coloring the graphic story.

Share your completed work with the class.